save the . . .
RHINOCEROSES

by **Sarah L. Thomson**
with an introduction
by **Chelsea Clinton**

PHILOMEL

PHILOMEL
An imprint of Penguin Random House LLC, New York

First published in the United States of America by Philomel,
an imprint of Penguin Random House LLC, 2023

Text copyright © 2023 by Chelsea Clinton

Photo credits: page 3: © Ludwig/Adobe Stock; page 5: © EcoView/Adobe Stock; page 7:
© Sandeep/Adobe Stock; page 9: © Erich/Adobe Stock; page 10: © slowmotiongli/Adobe
Stock; page 17: © Mark Kostich/Adobe Stock; page 19: © Tony Baggett/Adobe Stock; page
22: © Mark Kostich/Adobe Stock; page 26: © wayne/Adobe Stock; page 32: © Smithsonian
American Art Museum, Gift of John Gellatly; page 35: © xavier/Adobe Stock; page 37:
© terex/Adobe Stock; page 42: © Belikova Oksana/Adobe Stock; page 49: © Trevor Barrett;
page 51: © Mohamed Amin Foundation; page 54: © Robert McCullough/Adobe Stock

Philomel is a registered trademark of Penguin Random House LLC.
The Penguin colophon is a registered trademark of Penguin Books Limited.

Visit us online at PenguinRandomHouse.com.

Library of Congress Cataloging-in-Publication Data is available.

ISBN 9780593622667 (hardcover)
ISBN 9780593622674 (paperback)

1st Printing

Printed in the United States of America

LSCC

Edited by Talia Benamy and Jill Santopolo • Design by Lily Qian
Text set in Calisto MT Pro

save the . . .

save the . . .
BLUE WHALES

save the . . .
ELEPHANTS

save the . . .
FROGS

save the . . .
GIRAFFES

save the . . .
GORILLAS

save the . . .
KOALAS

save the . . .
LIONS

save the . . .
POLAR BEARS

save the . . .
RHINOCEROSES

save the . . .
TIGERS

save the . . .
WHALE SHARKS

Dear Reader,

When I was around your age, my favorite animals were dinosaurs and elephants. I wanted to know everything I could about triceratopses, stegosauruses and other dinosaurs that had roamed our earth millions of years ago. Elephants, though, captured my curiosity and my heart. The more I learned about the largest animals on land today, the more I wanted to do to help keep them and other endangered species safe forever.

So I joined organizations working around the world to support endangered species and went to our local zoo to learn more about conservation efforts close to home (thanks to my parents and grandparents). I tried to learn as much as I could about how we can ensure animals and plants don't go extinct like the dinosaurs, especially since it's the choices that we're making that pose the greatest threat to their lives today.

The choices we make don't have to be huge to make

a real difference. When I was in elementary school, I used to cut up the plastic rings around six-packs of soda, glue them to brightly colored construction paper (purple was my favorite) and hand them out to whomever would take one in a one-girl campaign to raise awareness about the dangers that plastic six-pack rings posed to marine wildlife around the world. I learned about that from a book—*50 Simple Things Kids Can Do to Save the Earth*—which helped me understand that you're never too young to make a difference and that we all can change the world. I hope that this book will inform and inspire you to help save this and other endangered species. There are tens of thousands of species that are currently under threat, with more added every year. We have the power to save those species, and with your help, we can.

Sincerely,

Chelsea Clinton

save the . . .
RHINOCEROSES

CONTENTS

-- -- -- -- -- -- -- -- -- -- -- -- --

1

GRASSLANDS, RIVERLANDS, AND ISLANDS: WHERE RHINOS LIVE

A rhino is pretty easy to spot if you're in the right place. Over a plain of gently waving grass, you might see a smooth gray back and catch a glimpse of a sharp horn—perhaps two. Or if you were hiking through a steamy rainforest, you could spy a mother and calf together, wallowing happily in a slippery mudhole.

You'd notice right away that rhinos are huge. When it comes to land animals, only elephants are bigger than the largest rhinos. And just like elephants, rhinos can be found in both Africa and Asia. There are five kinds, or species, of rhino alive today—two in Africa and three in Asia.

Rhinos in Africa

Black and white rhinos both live in Africa. The names can be confusing. Black rhinos are not black, and white rhinos are not white. They are actually both gray.

So where did their names come from?

Some people think that white rhinos got their name from an old Dutch word that means "wide" and sounds a little like the English word "white." Perhaps Dutch-speaking colonists in the country of South Africa saw these massive creatures and used this word to describe them.

Or perhaps they meant the word to apply to the rhino's lips. A white rhino is also called square-lipped because its upper lip is broad and smooth and, well, wide. A black rhino's upper

A white, or square-lipped, rhino is a grazer—a herbivore that mainly eats grass.

lip comes to a point in the middle, so they are sometimes called hook-lipped.

But there's no actual evidence that this is how white rhinos got their name. We don't really know why white rhinos are called white or why the black ones are called black—except that maybe it seemed logical to have black rhinos if you already had white ones.

Apart from their lips, black rhinos and white rhinos look a lot alike. Both have two horns— one large, one small—set in the center of their heads. And both are gigantic.

A male white rhino can weigh five thousand pounds, about as much as a pickup truck. It can grow up to fourteen feet long, the same length as a Volkswagen Beetle. A female is a bit smaller. Black rhinos are not quite as large— but even so, they're still enormous. The biggest

A black rhino is a browser, a herbivore that mainly eats the leaves, buds, shoots, and twigs that grow on trees and bushes.

ones can weigh close to four thousand pounds and grow up to twelve and a half feet long.

Both black and white rhinos are herbivores, or plant-eaters. But because their lips are shaped differently, they eat different things. White rhinos use their square lips to graze on short grasses, cropping them very close to the ground. They're almost like giant lawn mowers on legs. Black rhinos use their hooked lips to chop leaves, buds, shoots, and twigs off bushes and trees.

Since each species of rhino spends its time eating a different kind of plant, they can share the same habitat, which is a place that provides them with all they need to live. They both need somewhere warm where they can always find the kind of food they like best. That usually means a savanna, a grassy plain with a few trees and some bushes. Add in a source of water—such as a pond, a stream, a river, or a lake—and a rhino will be right at home.

Today most white rhinos live in South Africa. Black rhinos can be found there too, and also in Kenya, Namibia, and Zimbabwe.

Rhinos in Asia

In Asia you can find three species of rhino. The greater one-horned rhino is the biggest rhino in the world. It can reach a weight of six thousand pounds and grow to seven feet tall at its shoulder, which is higher than LeBron James

Its folds of skin make a greater one-horned rhino look a bit like it's wearing a suit of armor.

is tall. Its gray skin has folds that reach from its back to its belly.

As you can tell from the name, the greater one-horned rhino has just one horn. A rhino's horn continues to grow throughout its life, and the biggest of these rhinos can have horns up to two feet long.

The greater one-horned rhino is also called the Indian rhino, and it lives in—you guessed it—India. It can also be found just to the northeast, in Nepal, living on grasslands and plains near rivers. There these rhinos find the food they need, such as grass and plants that grow in water. Greater one-horned rhinos are good swimmers and are happy to wade or paddle through water to bite off a tasty mouthful of river weed.

If you left India and Nepal and traveled

Like its larger relative, a Javan rhino has only one horn as well as skin folds along its sides.

southeast over the ocean, you'd find the islands of Java and Sumatra, both part of Indonesia. That's where you'd have to go if you were looking for the last two species of rhino.

The Javan rhino is also called the lesser one-horned rhino. It looks a lot like a smaller version of the greater one-horned rhino.

The Sumatran rhino is the smallest of all and the only Asian rhino that has two horns. It's also the only living rhino to have hair all over its body. The other four species have a bit of hair around their ears and on the tips of their tails. (They use those tails as flyswatters to smack

Look closely along the belly and legs of this Sumatran rhino to see a fringe of dark fur.

away troublesome insects.) But the Sumatran rhino is covered from snout to rump in fur that is fuzzy and reddish brown when the animal is young. The fur turns black and bristly in adults.

Neither of these two island-dwelling rhinos lives in grasslands or on a savanna like their larger relatives. They prefer moist, warm swamps and rainforests.

But no matter where they live, all rhinos have some things in common.

2

GRAZING AND WALLOWING:
WHAT RHINOS ARE LIKE

All rhinos are mammals, which means they are warm-blooded animals that don't lay eggs. Instead they give birth to babies that drink their mother's milk. (The two exceptions to this rule are the platypus and the echidna, which are mammals that lay eggs.) All rhinos are herbivores. They all have three toes on each foot. And of course, they all have horns.

The name *rhinoceros* comes from two old

Greek words: *rhino*, which means "nose," and *keros*, which means "horn." A rhino's horn is made of a protein called keratin, which is the same stuff that makes up your own hair and fingernails. The horns on most other animals have a core of bone, but a rhino's horn is keratin all the way through.

A rhino uses its horn to dig up roots or to break down branches to eat. African rhinos use their horns to fight off dangerous animals, including other rhinos. Asian rhinos are different—they have tusks, long teeth that poke out of the sides of their mouths. They mostly use their tusks, rather than their horns, for fighting.

A horn is a very useful tool—but horns can also create problems for rhinos. You'll find out more about that in chapter 3.

Mostly Alone

Horses live in herds, and so do elephants. Lions live in prides. Several kinds of whales live in pods. But most rhinos do not. Black, greater one-horned, Javan, and Sumatran rhinos are solitary animals, which means they spend their lives alone, except when they are very young.

Young rhinos grow up with their mothers. But when they become adults, between two and four years old, they move on to live by themselves. Maybe they'll meet up with other rhinos at a watering hole now and then, or share a tasty patch of grass or brush. But they don't live in herds that stay together at all times.

Each male rhino lives in a territory of his own. He spends a lot of his time patrolling that territory and making sure that most other males keep out. He may make an exception for one or two other males and allow them to stay, but those males don't get to mate with any females that wander in.

Females do not have a territory in the same way that males do. Instead, they have what is called a home range, a stretch of land where they spend most of their time. Females do not try to keep other rhinos out, and a female's range may overlap with the territory of more than one male. The males allow the females to travel where they want.

White rhinos, however, are different. Adult males are solitary, but females and the young do live in groups. Some groups are made up of mothers and their babies. Others may be made of young rhinos that are not related. As many as twelve white rhinos may spend their lives feeding, drinking, and resting together.

Whether they live in groups or alone, rhinos have to communicate. They have a number of different ways to let other rhinos know how they feel and what they want.

Talking Rhino

Male rhinos have to send a very important message to other males. It's this: "Stay out of my territory!"

The main way rhinos send this message is simple and smelly—by using urine and dung (also known as pee and poop).

A male rhino leaves piles of dung on the ground to mark the edges of his territory. Sometimes he'll have twenty to thirty of these piles and will come back to add to them over and over again. Often he'll scrape his hooves through the piles, flinging the smelly stuff far and wide.

If a rhino comes across a pile of dung left by another rhino, he will smell it carefully and often add his own to the heap, maybe as to announce, "I was here too!"

Male white rhinos also use urine to mark their territories, and they'll scrape the ground with their hooves and horns to leave marks behind.

A dung pile like this, used to mark a rhino's territory, is called a midden.

If one male ignores all of these signals and makes his way into another male's territory, he may find himself face-to-face with that other rhino. Now may be the time to use sound to communicate. A gruff roar is a good way to say, "Get out!" or "Keep away!" And if that doesn't work, one rhino may start what is called a bluff-and-bluster display.

The rhino will snort and swing its huge, heavy head, showing off its dangerous horn or horns. This show of strength may be enough to make the other rhino leave. But perhaps the second rhino will charge instead. If that happens, the blustering rhino will often gallop away, maybe turning back momentarily to bluff and bluster some more.

If bluffing and blustering doesn't scare one of the two rhinos away, it may be time for a

Sharp horns, long tusks (if they have them), heavy heads, and sheer size are a rhino's weapons.

fight. Rhinos charge at each other and shove with their enormous heads to drive an intruder away. African rhinos slash or stab with their horns, while all three types of Asian rhino use their tusks in a fight. If one rhino doesn't back off, these fights can become deadly.

This kind of fighting has made many people

believe that rhinos are dangerous, not just to other rhinos, but to human beings as well. It's often said that rhinos (especially black ones) will charge at anything, including people.

But the truth is, rhinos have very poor eyesight. They're easily startled by anything moving nearby and may charge at something simply because they don't know what it is. Rhinos have even been seen charging at trees and boulders!

In fact, rhinos mostly prefer to stay away from people. The best way for humans to be safe around rhinos—or any large animal—is to give them the space that they need.

Not all rhino communication is about fighting. Rhinos may lift their tails to show that they are curious or alarmed. They can scream or shriek if they are frightened. A young rhino may whine if it needs its mother. And a contented rhino will let out a long sound a bit like *mmmwonk* to show that all is well.

A Rhino's Day

A big animal like a rhino needs a lot of food. And that means eating is pretty much a rhino's full-time job. Most rhinos spend mornings, late afternoons, and evenings finding food and water. During the hottest part of the day, right in the middle, rhinos usually seek out a shady spot to rest. They may lie down to sleep, or they may snooze on their feet. Black rhinos tend to have particular spots—a hill with a few trees for shade, perhaps, or a nice hollow in a grassy plain—where they come back day after day to spend some time dozing.

Along with eating and resting, a rhino must do something else. It must wallow. If a rhino finds a water hole, a lake, or just a nice muddy spot, it will lie down and roll in the muck, making sure it's covered from ears to tail to toenails.

Rhinos wallow because their thick gray skin (also called their hide) is quite sensitive. It can be easily cut or scarred or sunburned, and insect bites can leave marks. Coating the skin in mud

A greater one-horned rhino enjoys a good wallow.

protects it. It also helps rhinos keep cool.

African rhinos have an extra way to protect themselves from bothersome insects. They get some help.

Oxpecker birds spend a lot of time with rhinos. They will come to perch on their backs and peck insects off rhinos' hides. Sometimes they even get the bugs that have crawled into rhinos' ears or nostrils. The birds do the same thing for other big grazing animals, including oxen. That's how they got their name.

Both animals get something they need. The birds get a meal. The rhinos get some relief from biting bugs. Oxpeckers also help rhinos in another way—they can warn of a threat nearby. If an oxpecker spots something and calls out in alarm, rhinos will often check out their surroundings to see what the danger might be.

What danger could threaten a rhino? The truth is, not much. The most dangerous thing to an adult rhino is another rhino—or a human being. You'll hear more about the problems humans can cause for rhinos in chapter 4.

But there are a few predators that can put a young rhino in danger.

How Baby Rhinos Grow Up

A baby rhino is called a calf (just like a baby cow). A female rhino can have her first calf when she is around five or six years old.

Most rhino mothers have one baby at a time. Every now and then twins are born, but this is pretty rare. Newborn calves have no horns. When they are a few months old, their horns begin to grow, and they slowly get larger and larger every year of the rhinos' lives.

At birth, a baby rhino can weigh as little as 60 pounds (about the size of an adult golden retriever) or as much as 140 pounds (like a grown Saint Bernard). The calf will quickly grow bigger, and it needs a lot of food to make that happen.

Like all mammals, rhino calves drink their mother's milk. They'll get their first sip just a few hours after they're born, and they will keep on nursing for a year or a year and a half. But they also start to nibble on grass or leaves when they are just a few weeks or perhaps a month old.

Mothers keep their calves close. A female rhino will put herself between her calf and a threat, and she'll drive off anything she thinks might be a danger—including another rhino. A mother keeps a watchful eye out for predators. Hyenas, lions, tigers, and crocodiles will make a meal out of a calf if they get the chance.

A greater one-horned rhino calf snuggles close to its mother.

Calves stay with their mothers for two or three or maybe four years. If there is another calf nearby, the two may play by pushing each other gently with their horns or tossing their heads the way adult rhinos do to show their strength and power. Calves also play by themselves, prancing or running in circles.

When a calf is old enough to survive on its own, its mother will stop caring for it. If a female rhino is getting ready to have another baby, she will often chase her older calf away before the new one is born. The young rhino might go on to live by itself, or it might find another female that will watch over it for a while. White rhino calves sometimes gather in groups with others around their own age.

When it is between two and four years old, a calf has reached its adult size or very close to it. It can usually take care of itself against any threat—except for a human being.

3

POACHERS, VOLCANOES, AND NOT ENOUGH SPACE: WHY RHINOS ARE ENDANGERED

The International Union for Conservation of Nature (IUCN) keeps track of animal species all over the world. Its Red List of Threatened Species™ puts animals into seven different categories:

Least Concern: This animal is doing all right. There are enough healthy animals to have enough healthy babies to keep the species going.

Near Threatened: This animal is not in

trouble yet, but there are danger signs. It may become Vulnerable, Endangered, or Critically Endangered soon.

Vulnerable: There are not many of this animal left. Its numbers are falling, and it can live only in certain small areas. It is at risk of extinction.

Endangered: This animal is at high risk of extinction.

Critically Endangered: This animal is at very high risk of extinction.

Extinct in the Wild: This animal lives only in captivity. There are none left in the wild.

Extinct: This animal is gone forever.

White rhinos can be divided into two kinds—southern and northern. Today there are only two northern white rhinos left alive, a female named Sudan and her daughter, Najin. Southern white rhinos are doing better, thanks to a lot of hard work you'll soon read about. On the Red List, both kinds of white rhino are counted as one group and listed as Near Threatened.

Greater one-horned rhinoceroses are listed as Vulnerable.

Black rhinos are in peril as a species. They are Critically Endangered—the last step before being considered extinct in the wild. There are about 5,500 left alive.

Sumatran and Javan rhinos are in even more trouble. There are fewer than one hundred of each living today. Both species are listed as Critically Endangered.

If you counted all the rhinos alive in the early 1900s, you would have come up with about 500,000. Today there are only about 27,000 rhinos in the world.

What has been happening to the rhinos?

Hunted for Horns

A rhino's horns help it find food. They protect it in a fight. But the horns also place a rhino in danger.

For thousands of years, human beings have done their best to get their hands on rhino horns. When a horn is cut and polished, it can be made into beautiful carvings with a warm, yellowish brown color. Rhino horns have been used to make everything from buttons, belt buckles, hairpins, and the handles of ceremonial daggers to decorations for the belts of kimonos.

People also use rhino horn as a kind of medicine. The horn can't actually help anyone who is sick, but there are people in many Asian countries (including China, Taiwan, Vietnam, and India) who believe that it can. When the horn is ground into powder, it can be swallowed. Some hope that the powder will cure a fever or a headache, stop vomiting, clear up a rash, or even cure cancer.

A drinking cup carved from a rhino horn.

Let's be clear—it can't. Rhino horn, remember, is made from a protein called keratin, the same stuff your hair and fingernails are made of. Chewing on your hair or swallowing a fingernail clipping won't make you better if you're sick. Neither will eating some powdered rhino horn.

But this belief is strong enough that many people will pay a lot of money for even a tiny bit of powdered rhino horn. An ounce of rhino horn is more than twice as expensive as an ounce of gold. And that means some people are willing to break the law to find rhino horns to sell. In 2011, thieves smashed open a glass case in a museum in Sweden and sawed the horns off a stuffed rhino inside it.

Other criminals go after living rhinos instead. This kind of illegal hunting is called poaching. Poaching has wiped out rhinos in many of the countries where they once lived.

Adult rhinos don't have many ways to defend themselves against poachers, who sometimes use night-vision goggles, helicopters, and high-powered rifles. Rhinos don't see well, and they may not spot a poacher getting close. They can't outrun a helicopter or a jeep. They don't hide if they feel threatened. Some rhinos return to the same resting spots day after day, which makes them easy targets. All a poacher has to do is wait there for a rhino to show up.

Most rhinos today live in protected parks and preserves where hunting is illegal. Park rangers try to keep poachers out. Specially trained four-person teams called rhino protection units patrol parks in Indonesia. They remove traps and snares and keep an eye out for poachers and are trying hard to keep the last few Sumatran and Javan rhinos alive.

Workers in some parks even put rhinos to sleep with tranquilizer darts and cut off their horns before poachers can get to them. When the animal wakes up, it is set free again, healthy but missing a horn. (The horn will grow back over time.)

If a rhino has no horn, a poacher has no reason to kill it. When scientists followed horn-less rhinos to check on them, they found that

Cutting off a rhino's horn doesn't hurt the animal, just like getting your fingernails trimmed doesn't hurt you.

they survived just as well as rhinos with horns.

But rangers can't cut off every horn or keep an eye on every rhino. As long as people are willing to pay a lot of money for horns, poachers will find ways to kill rhinos.

And although it's important to have parks and preserves where rhinos can live safely, these protected areas can come with problems of their own.

Too Many Rhinos, Too Little Space

Rhinos are big animals, and big animals need space. They need a lot of land where the plants they eat each day can grow. And territorial animals, like male rhinos, need enough room so each male can have a territory of his own. That prevents fights between rhinos, which can be deadly.

Crowding rhinos too close together means higher risk for disease and fewer healthy calves.

People need space too. They need farmland to grow the crops they eat. They need pasture for animals like goats, sheep, and cows. They need space for houses, schools, factories, shops, roads, sidewalks, and train tracks.

But the more land that people take up, the less there is for rhinos.

When cities, towns, and farms grow too large, not much space is left as wilderness where rhinos and other animals can live. Protected areas for rhinos may be small, and a small park can support only a few rhinos. This is a problem on its own because we need parks that can support as many rhinos as possible. And it also means that the rhinos in those small parks are probably closely related. If rhinos that are close relatives mate, their calves are not likely to be healthy.

In a small space, rhinos spend more time near other rhinos. This means that disease can more easily spread from one rhino to another and to another, putting all of them in danger.

And finally, if too many rhinos are crammed into too little space, the females tend to have fewer calves. It's best for female rhinos to have as many calves as possible so these babies can grow up to have calves of their own. Crowding rhinos into small areas makes it less likely that this will happen.

So rhinos need more than just protected space. They need protected space that's big enough for them to spread out, find the right mates, and raise lots of calves. But this can only happen if we humans are willing to take a little less land for ourselves.

Natural Disasters

The few remaining Sumatran rhinos are scattered across the island of Sumatra. On the nearby island of Java, in the Ujung Kulon National Park, you can find the last Javan rhinos left alive.

These two species have to deal with all the

threats other rhino species face, plus another—natural disasters.

Of course, disasters like hurricanes or tidal waves or forest fires can be tough on any kind of animal. But even if many creatures are killed, there are usually survivors that can find mates and have young. The species will keep going.

That might not be the case for Javan and Sumatran rhinos. There are so few left, a single disaster could be just that—a disaster. If even a few rhinos are killed in a hurricane, or starve because a tidal wave swamps the land where their food grows, the species might not be able to recover.

That's a particular problem for Javan rhinos, because if you stand on the beach at Ujung Kulon and look across the ocean, you might see a smoky haze drifting from a volcano.

In fact, the whole reason Ujung Kulon exists as a national park at all is because of a volcano. In 1883, a nearby volcano, Krakatau (sometimes called Krakatoa), blew up in an eruption so loud and powerful, it could be heard two thousand miles away. Tsunamis, or tidal waves, the biggest more than a hundred feet above the level of the sea, slammed into nearby islands. The area where Ujung Kulon now exists was buried in ash and dust. The land was left to return to wilderness, and that wilderness was made into a national park.

Krakatau blew itself apart with the force of the eruption. Another volcano rose where the old one once stood. It's called Anak Krakatau.

Scientists cannot say exactly when, but it's very likely that Anak Krakatau will erupt one day. If it does, it may well set off a tsunami

Smoke rises from the volcano Anak Krakatau, whose name means "Child of Krakatau."

racing across the ocean toward Ujung Kulon. A wave just ten feet high could wipe out 80 percent of the rhino habitat in the park, making life even harder for the very few Javan rhinos that remain.

Considering the threats rhinos face—poachers, people who are eager to buy medicine and ornaments made of rhino horn, crowding, loss of their habitats, and volcanoes on the horizon—it's amazing they have survived so long. Part of the reason they have done so is that many people have been working hard to keep rhinos from vanishing forever.

4

SCIENTISTS, RHINO MOMS, AND MORE: WHO HAS BEEN SAVING RHINOS?

Human beings have poached rhinos even though it's against the law. We have taken over so much land that rhinos are crowded into spaces too small for them. We've made it hard for rhinos to survive. But we can also help them if we try.

Frozen Zoo

You've probably visited a zoo at least once.

Maybe you've even seen a rhino there. But you've never seen a zoo like the Frozen Zoo, which is run by the San Diego Zoo Wildlife Alliance.

The Frozen Zoo doesn't keep animals in habitats where visitors can see and admire them. Instead, it keeps cells taken from the bodies of many different animals. It has collected over ten thousand samples of cells. Some of them are from rhinos, including the northern white rhino.

You already know that there are only two northern white rhinos left alive—a mother and a daughter. With no male living, there's no chance for either of the two females to have any calves.

But the Frozen Zoo may still be able to help.

The zoo has skin cells from twelve different northern white rhinos. Scientists at the zoo are doing experiments to see if these skin cells can be transformed into a different kind of cell—a stem cell. Stem cells could then be combined to create embryos, which can grow to become babies. A southern white rhino female might be able to carry a northern white rhino embryo inside her until she is ready to give birth.

The process is complex and difficult, but scientists are hopeful that if it works, they could possibly bring the northern white rhino back from the very edge of extinction.

Safe New Homes

Without the help of scientists like those at the Frozen Zoo, northern white rhinos may become extinct very soon. More than a hundred years ago, though, it was their close relatives, the southern white rhinos, that seemed on the road to extinction. In fact, as the nineteenth century drew to a close, most people believed there were no southern white rhinos left.

Then, in 1895, a hundred southern white rhinos were discovered in the KwaZulu-Natal province in South Africa.

People began trying to figure out how to save these last few southern white rhinos. A protected area, the Hluhluwe Umfolozi Game Reserve (now called Hluhluwe-iMfolozi Park), was set up to keep them safe from poachers. By 1953 there were more than four hundred white rhinos there. But that wasn't enough to be sure the species would be protected from extinction. Two men who worked at Hluhluwe Umfolozi dedicated themselves to making sure the southern white rhino would survive.

Ian Player, who was white, was a game

warden at the reserve. Magqubu Ntombela, who was Black and a member of the Zulu people, worked there as a guide. At that time, the government of South Africa practiced what they called apartheid, which means apartness or separation. White people and Black people were kept strictly apart, and Black people had fewer opportunities and rights. Nice houses, good jobs, education, political power—all of these were pretty much reserved for white people. This terrible policy continued until the early 1990s.

Despite the injustice of apartheid, Player and Ntombela formed a close partnership. During the 1950s and 1960s, they worked together on Operation Rhino, a plan to capture southern white rhinos and transport them to parks, preserves, and zoos all over the world. This gave

Ian Player and Magqubu Ntombela worked together to keep the southern white rhino from extinction.

the rhinos the space they needed. It allowed them to find mates and have healthy calves that would grow up to have calves of their own.

Operation Rhino was a success. Today there are about 16,000 southern white rhinos in the world, more than any other rhino species.

Walking for Rhinos

Michael Werikhe grew up in Mombasa, Kenya. When he was an adult, he got a job with Kenya's Game Department, working to record and organize goods the government had seized from poachers—things like elephant tusks, animal skins, and rhino horns.

But Werikhe didn't feel that he was doing enough in this job to help animals—especially rhinos. So in 1982, he decided to try something else. He set out to walk three hundred miles between the cities of Mombasa and Nairobi, talking to everyone he met along the way about the dangers rhinos were facing and what could be done to save them.

Three years later, he did another walk, this one more than a thousand miles, through the countries of Uganda, Kenya, and Tanzania.

Later walks took him through several European countries, the United States, and Taiwan.

Everywhere he went, Werikhe talked to people—sometimes giving speeches, sometimes simply chatting with passersby. He was convinced that it was not possible for governments to save endangered animals like rhinos unless everyday people understood what was

Michael Werikhe and a rhino calf walking together to spread the word about what we must do to save rhinos from extinction.

happening to these animals and what they could do to help. "The man in the street is very willing to conserve wildlife, as long as he has information and does not feel left out," he told an interviewer.

Werikhe got the nickname "the Rhino Man." His walks taught an untold number of people about rhinos and how to save them. He also raised money, donated by people who were impressed by his efforts and wanted to help. The money was used by the government of Kenya to build parks and preserves to keep rhinos safe.

A Home for Orphans

When poachers kill any rhino, it's a great loss for the species. But when poachers kill a mother with a calf, that loss is even greater. Most rhino

calves won't live long without a mother to protect them.

The Rhino Orphanage in South Africa is
working to change that. It offers a safe place for
orphaned rhino calves to grow up. Many of the
calves at the orphanage had mothers that were
killed by poachers. Others are there because
their mothers died from injuries, illness, or a
fight with another rhino. (Female rhinos do not
fight as often as males do, but it does happen
sometimes—for example, a mother may be
injured while protecting her calf from a male.)

When workers at the orphanage get a call
that a mother rhino has died and her calf is in
trouble, they spring into action. First they have
to find the baby rhino. Calves younger than
five months tend to stay near the bodies of
their mothers, but older calves may run away. It

A rhino calf in the wild will not survive long on its own.

can take a few days to track them down.

When the calves are found, they are given a drug that makes them sleepy. Blindfolds are wrapped around their heads and ear plugs are put into their ears. This helps to keep them calm during the ride to the orphanage.

At the orphanage, the calf is offered its first bottle of milk. As it drinks, the blindfold is taken off. The calf learns to connect the idea of food with the smell and touch of a human being. This helps it learn to trust its caretakers.

Each calf has one person who takes care of it full time. A rhino "mom" stays near the calf, cuddling and stroking it. Calves in the wild are used to being near their mothers most of the time. The human touch and contact help them feel safe.

Once a calf is comfortable and calm, it can be taken outside. To avoid any fights, calves are not introduced to other rhinos right away. Instead, they may be offered a lamb or a goat to keep them company. The orphanage also has guard dogs that keep watch for poachers who might want to harm the rhino calves. These dogs are sometimes companions for a young calf as well.

After the calves settle into their new home, they begin to spend time with other young rhinos. They are taken on walks where they can nibble leaves or grass. Their human moms continue to feed them from bottles until they are a year and a half or maybe two years old.

After the calves are too old to drink from bottles, their caretakers begin to spend less and less time with them. Instead, the calves spend their days with other rhinos. This helps to keep them from depending on people for food or comfort as they grow to adulthood.

When they reach four or five years old, the young rhinos are ready to be released back into the wild. The Rhino Orphanage keeps track of the rhinos it has raised to make sure they survive and hopefully grow up to have calves of their own.

Sniffing to Save Endangered Species

Their names are Kira, Tivo, Diva, and Ram. Together they are the Kenya Wildlife Service Canine Unit. By doing what comes naturally to dogs—sniffing—they are helping to protect other animals from extinction.

These four dogs have been trained to detect the smell of rhino horns, elephant tusks, and pangolin scales, which are the animal parts that poachers most often try to smuggle out of Kenya. You already know why people poach rhinos for their horns. Elephants are often killed for their tusks, which can be carved and polished and turned into ivory. Pangolins are scaly animals a little like anteaters and are hunted for their meat. It is considered a rare treat or a delicacy. And many people believe their scales can be made into medicine, just like a rhino horns.

The dogs work at places like the Moi International Airport and the Kilindini Harbour in Mombasa, a large city in Kenya. They sniff suitcases and packages going on planes and check out giant containers that will be packed onto ships.

If the dogs catch the scent of horns, tusks, or scales, they sit down right away to let their handlers know they've found something. The Wildlife Service will then make sure the horns, tusks, or scales don't leave the country. That means no one will make money selling rhino horns or anything else from an endangered animal.

Safe from Disasters

As you know, the Javan rhinos in the Ujung Kulon National Park risk being wiped out if Anak Krakatau erupts or if any other natural disaster strikes. The World Wildlife Fund, Indonesia's Ministry of Environment, and the International Rhino Foundation are working to change that. They hope to find a second home for Javan rhinos. If half of the remaining rhinos stay in Ujung Kulon and half live elsewhere, there's a better chance the species will survive a tsunami, hurricane, or earthquake. Two homes would mean that the species has twice the chance of survival.

Sniffing suitcases and containers. Finding new homes for rhinos and raising orphaned calves. Walking and talking and telling as many people as possible about what needs to be done to save rhinos from extinction. There are so many ways to help rhinos and other endangered animals. If we all find at least one small thing to do, there's still hope that we can live in a world that will always have rhinos in it.

FUN FACTS ABOUT RHINOS

1. A rhino can gallop at thirty miles per hour—about as fast as a car driving down a neighborhood street. But they can only do this for a short amount of time.

2. A greater one-horned rhino can drop a pile of dung that weighs as much as fifty-five pounds. That's about as heavy as an average American seven-year-old kid.

3. A rhino's ears can move in different directions at the same time. One may point forward to catch a sound up ahead

while the other tips backward to check out something behind.

4. A group of rhinos can be called a crash.

5. Male rhinos are called bulls. Females are cows.

6. A black rhino can go for five days without drinking water. It will get all the liquid it needs from plants.

7. The largest rhino horn ever measured was fifty-nine inches long. That's about a yard and a half—longer than a standard doorway is wide!

8. When scientists are studying rhinos, they often look for the dung left behind. It can tell them what a rhino has been eating and where it has traveled. But elephants and rhinos often live near each other, and scientists have to be sure not

to confuse the two kinds of dung. One way to tell them apart is to look for the two grooves made by a rhino's hooves as it scrapes its back feet through the dung. Elephants don't scrape. They just leave their dung where it falls.

9. Today there are only five species of rhino in the world. But nearly one hundred species have existed over time. The wooly rhino once lived in North America, Europe, and Asia. It had two horns and was covered with a thick coat of dark hair. Early humans made paintings of it on cave walls, which can still be seen today. The Chauvet Cave in France has about sixty wooly rhino images on its walls.

10. "Rhinoceros beetle" is a name used to

describe several species of insects. The males have a long horn or horns on their heads that look a lot like the horn of a rhino. Some rhinoceros beetles can grow up to six inches long and can lift things 850 times their own weight. They may look fierce, but they are harmless plant-eaters.

HOW YOU CAN HELP SAVE THE RHINOS

There are a lot of things you can do to help save the rhinos. Here are a few of them:

1. Visit a zoo to learn more about rhinos and other animals. Many zoos have conservation programs to help study and protect endangered animals. When you pay money to visit a zoo, you're helping to support that important work. You can visit the Association of Zoos and Aquariums at Aza.org to make sure you are spending your money at a zoo where animals like rhinos get the best possible treatment.

2. Explain to everyone you know why you should never buy anything made from rhino horn. If you see something for sale, maybe when you are on vacation, and wonder if it might be made of rhino horn (or ivory from an elephant's tusks or anything else from an endangered animal), ask someone working at the store where it came from. If they can't tell you—don't buy it! Poachers can't make money selling rhino horns if no one buys them.

3. Let people know that rhino horns don't work as medicine.

4. Find out more about rhinos. These books are a good place to start:

*Rhino Rescue: Changing the
Future for Endangered Wildlife*
by Garry Hamilton

Emi and the Rhino Scientist
by Mary Kay Carson

*Rhino Rescue! And More
True Stories of Saving Animals*
by Clare Hodgson Meeker

*Rhino in the House:
The True Story of Saving Samia*
by Daniel Kirk

5. Adopt a rhino. Not to be a pet, though! Adopting an endangered animal means donating money to an organization such as Save the Rhino International or the World Wildlife Fund that works to protect rhinos and other animals. You can often get an adoption certificate with your donation and maybe even an adorable stuffed rhino.

6. You can also adopt an orphaned rhino calf at the Rhino Orphanage by sending money to help raise the calf and keep it safe. Visit TheRhinoOrphanage.org to find out more.

7. Does adopting a rhino seem too expensive? Maybe you can find a way to raise some money. What about setting up a stand to sell cookies, lemonade, art, or bracelets that you have made? Let people know you are donating the money you raise to help save endangered rhinos.

8. Ask for some help and you can raise even more money for rhinos. Your friends,

your family, your class, or a group like a scout troop can all work together to make even more money to help rhinos.

9. Have a rhino-themed birthday party. You could serve rhino-shaped cookies, have a scavenger hunt where participants discover rhino facts, and play pin the tail on the rhino. Instead of gifts, ask for donations to an organization, like the International Rhino Foundation, that works to save rhinos.

10. Write to the people who make laws and ask them to support laws and treaties against wildlife trafficking—which means selling animals or their body parts (such as rhino horns). Explain that you are worried about what poaching and trafficking will do to rhinos and other endangered animals if we don't take action. You may not be able to vote yet, but one day you will be. And that means that people who make the laws care about what you and kids like you think. You can find out who to write to and how to contact them by visiting congress.gov/members/find-your-member.

11. When you are old enough to vote, use your vote to support leaders who will care for the environment and protect endangered animals like rhinos. (And until then, ask all the adults in your life who can vote to do so!)

REFERENCES

African Wildlife Foundation. "Rhinoceros."
    May 19, 2022. awf.org/wildlife
    -conservation/rhinoceros.

Barr, Cameron. "He'll Walk a Mile for a
    Rhino." *Christian Science Monitor*,
    June 11, 1991. csmonitor.com/1991
    /0611/11141.html.

Daley, Jason. "Sniffer Dogs Represent the
    Latest Weapon in the Fight Against
    the Illegal Ivory Trade." Smithsonian,
    August 28, 2018. smithsonianmag.com

/smart-news/sniffer-dogs-and-new
-technology-team-save-elephants
-180970143/.

The Goldman Environmental Prize. "1990
Goldman Prize Winner: Michael
Werikhe." Accessed May 26, 2022.
goldmanprize.org/recipient/michael
-werikhe/#recipient-bio.

History. "This Day in History: August 27,
1883; Krakatoa Explodes." Accessed July
18, 2022. history.com/this-day-in-history
/krakatau-explodes.

International Rhino Foundation. "The
Rhino Family." Accessed June 6, 2022.
rhinos.org/about-rhinos/rhino-species/.

Martin, Douglas. "Ian Player Is Dead at 87;
Helped to Save Rhinos." *The New York*

Times, December 3, 2014. nytimes.com /2014/12/04/world/africa/ian-player -conservationist-who-helped-save-white -rhinos-dies-at-87.html.

National Geographic. "Black Rhinoceros." Accessed May 31, 2022.

National Geographic Kids. "Rhino Facts! These Animals Are Big, Bulky and Absolutely Brilliant!" Accessed May 25, 2022. natgeokids.com/uk/discover/animals /general-animals/rhinoceros-facts/.

Orenstein, Ronald. *Ivory, Blood, and Horn: Behind the Elephant and Rhinoceros Poaching Crisis.* Buffalo, NY: Firefly Books, 2013.

"Rhinoceros Fact Sheet." *Nature*. PBS: PBS Thirteen, August 27, 2020. pbs.org/wnet /nature/blog/rhinoceros-fact-sheet/.

The Rhino Orphanage. "Giving Rhino
Orphans a Future." Accessed July 20,
2022. therhinoorphanage.org.

Rogers, Peter. "Northern White Rhino:
Resurrecting an Extinct Species in Four
Steps." Big Think, March 22, 2022.
bigthink.com/life/resurrection
-deextinction-northern-white-rhino/.

San Diego Zoo Wildlife Alliance: Animals
and Plants. "Rhinoceros." Accessed May
25, 2022. animals.sandiegozoo.org
/animals/rhinoceros.

San Diego Zoo Wildlife Alliance Library.
"Black Rhinoceros (Diceros bicornis)
Fact Sheet." Accessed May 31, 2022.
ielc.libguides.com/sdzg/factsheets
/blackrhino/summary.

San Diego Zoo Wildlife Alliance Library. "White Rhinoceros (Ceratotherium simum) Fact Sheet." Accessed May 19, 2022. ielc.libguides.com/sdzg/factsheets/whiterhino.

San Diego Zoo Wildlife Alliance: Science. "Frozen Zoo." Accessed May 19, 2022. science.sandiegozoo.org/resources/frozen-zoo®.

San Diego Zoo Wildlife Alliance. "Take Action: Wildlife Trafficking." Accessed June 2, 2022. sandiegozoowildlifealliance.org/take-action/wildlife-trafficking.

"Taking Steps for Rhinos: The Odyssey of Michael Werikhe." *Zoonooz*, May 1991. docslib.org/doc/2148261/the-odyssey-of-michael-werikhe.

Torchia, Christopher. "Secret South African Orphanage Cares for Baby Rhinos." *Christian Science Monitor,* July 22, 2015. csmonitor.com/World/Making-a -difference/Change-Agent/2015/0722 /Secret-South-African-orphanage-cares -for-baby-rhinos.

Wild. "Who We Are: History." Accessed June 6, 2022. wild.org/who-we-are /history/.

World Wildlife Fund. "Black Rhino: Facts." Accessed May 23, 2022. worldwildlife .org/species/black-rhino.

World Wildlife Fund. "Greater One-Horned Rhino: Facts." Accessed May 23, 2022. worldwildlife.org/species/greater-one -horned-rhino.

World Wildlife Fund. "Sumatran Rhino: Facts." Accessed May 23, 2022. worldwildlife.org/species/sumatran-rhino.

SARAH L. THOMSON has published more than thirty books, including prose and poetry, fiction and nonfiction, picture books, and novels. Her work includes two adventures featuring a teenage-girl ninja; a riveting survival story about wildfires and wombats; and nonfiction about elephants, sharks, tigers, plesiosaurs, saber-toothed cats, and other fascinating creatures. *School Library Journal* called Sarah's picture book *Cub's Big World* "a big must-have." *The Bulletin of the Center for Children's Books* described her novel *Deadly Flowers* as "clever, dangerous, vivacious," and *Booklist* said this fantasy set in feudal Japan is "genuinely thrilling, with surprises at every turn and a solid emotional core." *Deadly Flowers* also received Wisconsin's Elizabeth Burr/Worzalla award. Sarah worked as an editor at HarperCollins and Simon & Schuster before becoming a full-time writer. She lives in Portland, Maine.

Learn more about her work at
SarahLThomson.com

CHELSEA CLINTON is the author of the #1 *New York Times* bestseller *She Persisted: 13 American Women Who Changed the World*; *She Persisted Around the World: 13 Women Who Changed History*; *She Persisted in Sports: American Olympians Who Changed the Game*; *Don't Let Them Disappear: 12 Endangered Species Across the Globe*; *It's Your World: Get Informed, Get Inspired & Get Going!*; *Start Now!: You Can Make a Difference*; with Hillary Clinton, *Grandma's Gardens* and *The Book of Gutsy Women: Favorite Stories of Courage and Resilience*; and, with Devi Sridhar, *Governing Global Health: Who Runs the World and Why?* She is also the Vice Chair of the Clinton Foundation, where she works on many initiatives, including those that help empower the next generation of leaders. She lives in New York City with her husband, Marc, their children and their dog, Soren.

You can follow Chelsea Clinton on Twitter
@ChelseaClinton
or on Facebook at
Facebook.com/ChelseaClinton

DON'T MISS MORE BOOKS IN THE

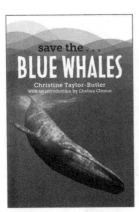

save the . . .
BLUE WHALES
Christine Taylor-Butler
With an introduction by Chelsea Clinton

save the . . .
ELEPHANTS
Sarah L. Thomson
With an introduction by Chelsea Clinton

save the . . .
FROGS
Sarah L. Thomson
With an introduction by Chelsea Clinton

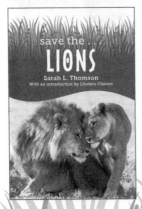

save the . . .
LIONS
Sarah L. Thomson
With an introduction by Chelsea Clinton

save the . . .
POLAR BEARS
Christine Taylor-Butler
With an introduction by Chelsea Clinton

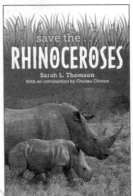

save the . . .
RHINOCEROSES
Sarah L. Thomson
With an introduction by Chelsea Clinton

save the... SERIES!

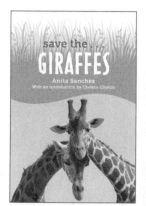

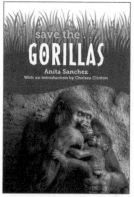

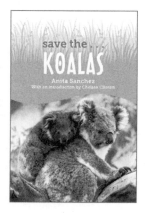

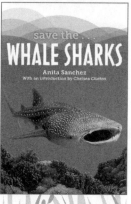